RL 6.8

Pts 1

D1548241

FAMOUS MOVIE MONSTERS™

INTRODUCING

IT CAME FROM OUTER SPACE

The Rosen Publishing Group, Inc.,
New York

SIMONE PAYMENT

Published in 2007 by The Rosen Publishing Group, Inc.
29 East 21st Street, New York, NY 10010

First Edition

Library of Congress Cataloging-in-Publication Data

Payment, Simone.
Introducing it came from outer space/Simone Payment.
   p. cm.—(Famous movie monsters)
Filmography:
Includes bibliographical references and index.
ISBN 1-4042-0826-7 (library binding)
1. It came from outer space (Motion picture) I. Title: It came from outer space. II. Title. III. Series.
PN1997.I755P39 2006
791.43'72—dc22

                                        2005033717

Manufactured in Malaysia

On the cover: The alien from *It Came from Outer Space*

CONTENTS

CHAPTER 1

IT CAME FROM OUTER SPACE

It is a late spring night in the desert town of Sand Rock, Arizona. John Putnam, a science fiction writer who lives in Sand Rock, is finishing a late dinner with his girlfriend, Ellen Fields, at his house. When they go outside to watch the night skies with John's telescope, they see a startling sight. A burning ball crashes to the earth and explodes. They believe it is a huge meteor.

However, the fiery ball is not a meteor. Instead, it is a large, round, glowing object. At the crash site, smoke swirls around a door that opens on one side. Except for some glowing lights, it is completely dark inside. Suddenly, a hideous monster with one eye emerges from the smoke. It exits its spacecraft and surveys the crash site.

The next morning John and Ellen hire their friend Pete to take them up in his helicopter so they can investigate the strange object. When they arrive at the crash site, John goes down into the crater to take a closer look. The crash-landed object is large and round, and it is covered with a pattern of hexagons.

One of the hexagons is a door, and it's open. Just as John gets close to the opening, a sudden avalanche of rocks and dust buries the object. John just barely escapes. He isn't sure what he saw, but he believes it may have been a spaceship. Pete and Ellen don't believe him and can't wait to get away from the crash site. However, John is sure he saw something.

"What would you say if I had found a Martian down there?" asks John. Pete and Ellen beg John not to tell anyone about what he saw. They believe people will think he's crazy.

John doesn't take their advice. He tells Matt, the town sheriff, that there's a spaceship buried in the crater. The sheriff doesn't believe him, but John remains convinced.

As John and Ellen drive home, they nearly hit something floating above the road. They get out of the car to investigate, but they see nothing. Hidden from sight, the monster watches them as they drive away. John and Ellen are unaware that they narrowly escaped an encounter with the alien.

The next day, the crater swarms with people taking photographs. Reporters crowd around John and ask him questions about what he saw the day before. No one believes that John has seen something from space. His story is just too outlandish for them. They believe he is either crazy or just imagining things.

As John and Ellen drive away from the site, they come upon Frank and George, two telephone linemen hard at work. Frank and George inform John and Ellen that they have been hearing weird noises in the wires. John listens for himself but is not sure of what it could be. Frank and George decide to try listening to the wires further up the road. On their way, they crash

John Putnam (Richard Carlson) stands before what he believes is a ship from outer space. Moments later, it is buried by an avalanche. John is only an amateur astronomer, but he is fairly certain that what he saw streaking through the sky before the crash was not a meteor. When he sees the open door in the side of the object, he is convinced that it is something other than a rock from space.

into a monster with a huge, vein-covered eye. The two men try to escape but are followed into the desert by the monster.

In the meantime, John and Ellen are headed in the opposite direction. Suddenly, John thinks he hears something, and he turns the car around to investigate. They come upon Frank and George's empty truck and walk into the desert to investigate.

Unbeknownst to John and Ellen, George has been following them. When George catches up to them, he acts very strange. He speaks in an odd, stiff voice and stares directly at the sun.

Ellen and John are suspicious of George and think there is something wrong with him. John sees an arm behind a nearby rock and suspects that Frank may be dead. John and Ellen hurry away from their strange meeting with George.

George walks back into the desert where we see Frank lying on the ground, just waking up. Frank starts talking to his friend but is mystified to see a second George lying on the ground, also just waking up. The real George is equally baffled by his double, who is standing over them. George's double tells the men not to be afraid. "It is within our power to transform ourselves to look like you. Or anyone. For a time, it will be necessary. We cannot, we would not, take your souls, or minds, or bodies," he says in a strange, inexpressive voice. "Don't be afraid. Your friend is all right," the alien tells them as he walks away.

After their odd encounter with George's double, John and Ellen hurry to the sheriff's office. They bring the sheriff with them into the desert. When they get to the place where George and Frank's truck was parked, the truck is gone. Frank and George are gone as well. The sheriff, again, doesn't believe them.

When John and Ellen go back to town, they talk about the strange things that have happened. Ellen says that it would be impossible for George to stare into the sun without blinking, as he did when they saw him in the desert. John agrees. Suddenly, they see George and Frank walking down the street. John jumps out of the car and calls to them, but they ignore him. Following

In this scene, John confronts the alien doubles of George and Frank in an alley. In some shots from this scene, you can see the shadow of the microphone used during filming. Sometimes called a boom mic, this type of microphone is attached to a pole and is held above the actors during filming to capture the dialogue.

them into an alley, he sees them enter a doorway. When he pushes the door open, George and Frank are standing in the shadows. They tell him to keep away. John tells them that he wants to help them, whomever they are.

"Then keep away. Keep away, John Putnam. We don't want to hurt you. We don't want to hurt anyone," they say to him. They tell him his friends are alive and ask him to just give them some time. If he doesn't, they say, "terrible things will happen. Things so terrible you have yet to dream of them."

Later that night, Ellen and John are asked to go to the sheriff's office. They learn that George and Frank have been reported missing. The sheriff admits that other strange things have been happening as well. George and Frank's truck, which was loaded with electrical equipment, is missing, and someone broke into the hardware store and stole some copper wire and other materials. As he is telling Ellen and John about these thefts, the sheriff gets a report. A scientist and his assistant who were investigating the crater are missing as well. The sheriff begins to believe that John may be right. Something strange is going on.

As Ellen drives home from town, she nearly runs over Frank, who is standing in the middle of the road. When she stops for him, Frank gets into Ellen's car and asks her to take him to the old mine. Frank isn't whom he appears to be, however. Ellen screams as the alien transforms back into its true form.

Back in the sheriff's office, John gets a mysterious phone call telling him that "they" have gotten Ellen. He is told to go to the desert. John hurries to the desert and waits there all night. In the morning he sees Ellen. She is standing on a hill and does not speak to him, and it is soon clear that she is not Ellen at all.

"Ellen" leads him into an old mine near the crater. As he stands in front of the entrance, John hears a voice. The voice tells John the aliens are trying to repair their ship so they can leave Earth that night. The voice asks John for his help, but John says, "How can I when you've kidnapped and stolen, for all I know even murdered?"

"We are good," the voice tells him. When John asks why they are hiding, the voice says, "We are not yet ready to meet in friendship . . . [Y]ou would be horrified at the sight of us. Had you fallen on our world it might have been different. We understand more."

The voice goes on to explain that they are holding Ellen and the other townspeople hostage. It warns that everyone should stay away and leave them alone to work on their ship. "Our mission was to another world. You must believe me. Only an error dragged us toward Earth."

The voice says that his people and the people of Earth should stay apart, or terrible destruction may occur. John refuses to listen to any more if the monster is unwilling to face him. The monster agrees to come out and emerges slowly. John looks on in shock, covering his eyes at the hideous sight. He staggers back into the desert and tells the sheriff about seeing the monster. The sheriff wants to go back for Ellen and the others but John begs him not to go. John tells the sheriff that the monsters have been hiding behind the "masks" of other people because the people of Earth destroy things they do not understand. The monsters understood this and took human form so humans would not kill them. John makes him understand that they will kill Ellen if he tries to interfere. The sheriff agrees to leave.

Later, the sheriff changes his mind. He decides he has to do something. He gathers men from the town to help him. John catches wind of the sheriff's plans and races to the mine, hoping to get there before the sheriff and his men do.

The alien doubles of the people of Sand Rock are shown here on a break from trying to repair their ship so they can leave Earth. Gun in hand, John Putnam pleads with the shape-shifting alien leader to let the people of Sand Rock go.

John arrives at the mine and enters. He sees Ellen's double and warns her that the sheriff's men are on their way. He says they've got to get out, but Ellen's double says the aliens need more time to finish their ship. The aliens no longer trust John. Just before Ellen's double points a ray gun at John, she says, "I'm sorry, we did not want to use violence. Now there's no

John stands in the desert with Ellen (Barbara Rush). Many science fiction movies are set in other times or strange lands. *It Came from Outer Space* was set in the present day and in a real environment. This made it easy for moviegoers to imagine how they would react if they were in the same situations as the characters.

other way." John quickly shoots, and Ellen's double falls off a cliff into a cavern below.

With the monster out of the way, John goes deeper into the mine. He discovers a huge room filled with machinery. Operating the machines are the doubles of John's friends—as well as a double of John! John's double explains that their machinery is powerful enough to destroy Earth. They had worked on it for thousands of years in order to travel to other planets.

John tells them that the sheriff and his men are on their way. He convinces the creatures that he'll help them get away by holding off the sheriff and his men. In return, the monsters must release Ellen and the others. The monsters aren't sure whether or not they can trust John, but they agree to let him try.

The monsters let Ellen and the others go with John. He leads them out of the mine. As they leave, the doubles turn back into their monster forms. When they get outside, John works to blow up the mine entrance, blocking the sheriff from entering. As the townspeople gather outside the mine, they hear and feel a distant rumbling. A fiery ball rises from the ground and streaks into the sky.

"Well, they're gone," says John.

"For good, John?" asks Ellen.

"No, just for now. It wasn't the right time for us to meet. But there'll be other nights, and other stars for us to watch. They'll be back," he replies.

CHAPTER 2

THE MAKING OF THE MOVIE

The people in the audience at the Pantages Theater in Hollywood, California, on May 26, 1953, were in for a treat. When the movie flickered onto the screen, haunting music began playing. They watched as a flaming ball streaked across the sky. Suddenly, the glowing object seemed to be coming directly at the audience, shooting out of the screen! As it exploded in a ball of fire, the words "It Came from Outer Space" filled the movie screen.

As the movie went on, the audience was in for an even greater shock. During the scene where an avalanche buries the spaceship, Styrofoam rocks shot into the crowd from catapults next to the movie screen, causing the audience to scream in fright and excitement. It was like nothing they'd ever seen before.

THE FIRST 3-D SCIENCE FICTION MOVIE

The excitement at the premiere of *It Came from Outer Space* was largely due to the

Moviegoers in the 1950s are shown here wearing 3-D glasses. In the early 1950s, 3-D movies such as the horror film *House of Wax* (1953) and the musical *Kiss Me Kate* (1953) were extremely popular. By the mid-1950s, 3-D movies had become less popular with theater owners, because they were difficult to show in the theater, and with moviegoers, who sometimes got headaches or tired eyes from watching them.

film's 3-D effects. *It Came from Outer Space* was not the first 3-D movie ever made, but it was the first science fiction movie to use the new technology. Short 3-D movies had been made as early as 1903, but it wasn't until the early 1950s that Hollywood began using 3-D technology to make feature films.

The abbreviation "3-D" is short for "three-dimensional." All objects have three dimensions: height, width, and depth. When you look at an image on a movie screen, you can usually only see two dimensions: height and width.

To create three-dimensional movies, filmmakers create two separate images. These two images are projected onto the screen at the same time, one tinted blue and the other tinted red. People viewing the images on the screen wear special glasses, which allow each eye to see only one of the images. In most cases, audiences watched 3-D films with glasses that had one red lens and one blue lens. The eye looking through the red lens sees the blue image on the screen. The eye looking through the blue lens sees the red image on the screen. The brain then combines these two images, allowing a viewer to perceive depth.

When *It Came from Outer Space* was released in 1953, 3-D was considered a new and exciting technology. Audiences were thrilled and amazed by the film's 3-D effects. In the beginning of the movie, the ball of fire seemed to be heading straight out of the screen. When the sheriff reached for his gun, his arm seemed to come straight toward the audience.

THE STORY

The Hollywood producer William Alland came up with the original idea for *It Came from Outer Space*. Alland imagined a movie in which an alien spacecraft crashed on Earth. The aliens would realize immediately that human beings were stupid and brutal. They would want to leave Earth as fast as possible, without hurting any humans. When he described his idea to Universal Studios, they approved it right away.

Alland wanted the author Ray Bradbury to write a story based on his movie idea. Alland would then take this story, called a treatment, and hire someone to turn it into a screenplay. Bradbury was already a well-known writer of science fiction stories and books. One of his most famous books, *The Martian Chronicles*, had been published in 1950. Alland paid Bradbury $3,000 for the treatment.

Bradbury ended up calling the story *Ground Zero, or The Atomic Monster*. Alland was very pleased with Bradbury's work. He thought they could make a movie directly from the story. However, Universal Studios decided to hire an experienced screenwriter named Harry

Jack Arnold *(right)* is pictured directing Grant Williams *(left)* in 1957's *The Incredible Shrinking Man*. In this classic science fiction movie, the hero begins to shrink after coming in contact with a radioactive cloud. As he grows smaller, he has to use his wits to avoid everyday dangers, such as the family cat.

Essex to adapt the story into a movie script. Bradbury's story was so well written that Essex did not have to do much work. Except for some additional dialogue, the final version of the script was nearly identical to Bradbury's story.

THE CAST AND CREW

The cast of *It Came from Outer Space* look on as the alien space ship takes off. Barbara Rush and Richard Carlson stand in the foreground, while *(from left to right)* Brad Jackson, George Eldredge, Russell Johnson, Alan Dexter, and Kathleen Hughes stand in the background.

Now that he had a finished screenplay, Alland needed a director and cast. He hired Jack Arnold to direct the movie. Arnold was born October 14, 1916, in New Haven, Connecticut. He began his career dancing and acting in Broadway plays during the 1930s and 1940s. During World War II (1939–1945) he made training films for the U.S. Army. In the early 1950s, Universal Studios recruited him to direct movies for the studio.

Alland and Universal chose Richard Carlson to star in *It Came from Outer Space*. Carlson was born in Albert Lea, Minnesota, on April 29, 1912. After graduating with honors from the University of Minnesota, Carlson had planned to become a teacher. Instead, he began acting in plays. Like Arnold, he starred in Broadway plays in the 1930s. The famous Hollywood producer David O. Selznik met Carlson in New York City. Selznik suggested Carlson go to Hollywood and become a writer and director. Once in Hollywood,

Carlson found work as an actor. He appeared in his first movie in 1938, *The Young in Heart*. Carlson then went overseas to serve in World War II and found it hard to get roles as an actor after the war. It wasn't until the 1950s that his acting career took off. Handsome and intelligent, Carlson was the perfect person to play John Putnam, the clever hero of *It Came from Outer Space*.

Barbara Rush was hired to play Ellen Fields. Born January 4, 1927, in Denver, Colorado, Rush had been acting since she was very young. She attended the University of California and appeared in a number of plays there. Rush went on to act at the Pasadena Playhouse in Pasadena, California, where she was discovered by Paramount Studios. She starred in a few movies for Paramount in the early 1950s. After the birth of her first child, Rush began working for Universal Studios. *It Came from Outer Space* was her first movie for Universal.

PREPARATION AND FILMING

Because *It Came from Outer Space* would be filmed in 3-D, the filmmakers had to do some tests. Film techniques for 3-D had existed for a number of years, but the technology could still be unpredictable. Before they started shooting the film, Jack Arnold wanted to see what kind of 3-D results they would get. So, two weeks before filming began, he had some of the actors do things like throw chairs toward the camera. When their 3-D footage looked as though it were popping out of the screen, they were ready to start filming the movie.

Most of *It Came from Outer Space* takes place in the desert, and the filmmakers were lucky to find a perfect filming location very close to Los Angeles. Most of the outdoor scenes of the movie were shot near Victorville, California. Victorville is in the Mojave Desert, less than two hours away from Los Angeles. Some scenes were filmed at Red Top Mountain, which is also located in the Mojave Desert.

Some outdoor scenes were shot right on Universal Studios' soundstages. The studio owned a set called Sierra Canyon, which was often used for filming Westerns. Sierra Canyon had a main street, which was used for the town scenes in *It Came from Outer Space*. Other scenes from *It Came from Outer Space* were filmed with painted backgrounds on Stage 12, the largest soundstage at Universal.

Guards were posted on the movie sets to keep the public out. The studio wanted to build interest for the movie, but at the same time they were trying to keep many aspects of the movie secret. They also wanted to keep other studios from copying their ideas. Universal worried that another studio might release a similar movie first and audiences would no longer be interested in going to see *It Came from Outer Space*.

CREATING THE SPECIAL EFFECTS

Watching *It Came from Outer Space* today, most of the special effects don't seem very exciting or advanced. For the time, however, the special effects were amazing: 3-D effects, such as the monster's eye coming out of the screen, thrilled 1950s audiences.

It Came from Outer Space was also the first movie that included scenes shot from the point of view of a monster. When the monster attacks Ellen, we see through the monster's eyes as it comes at her. The scenes shot from the monster's point of view include strange moving lights at the edges of the screen. To create this effect, the filmmakers began by putting oil in a bowl. They placed bright lights above the bowl and positioned the camera beneath the bowl so it could shoot through the oil. The bowl was jiggled so the lights would "dance" on the oil. They then superimposed this footage over scenes that showed the monster's perspective.

The flying spaceship shown in the very beginning of the movie was a hollow, metal ball about the size of a bowling ball. Shapes were cut out of the ball and it was attached to a wire. When they were ready to film the scene, they filled the hollow ball with magnesium powder, which they then set on fire. The magnesium powder burned very brightly as the ball was released. The ball was filmed in slow motion as it slid down the wire. The filmmakers wanted to show the ball crashing, but it couldn't crash directly into the camera. So, they had the ball head toward a mirror and filmed the ball's reflection. If you watch the movie carefully, you can see the mirror breaking as the ball hits it.

In some scenes, stand-ins were used in place of Carlson or Rush. Stand-ins are actors and actresses who look similar to the stars. They are used for scenes where you don't see the stars at close range.

For the scene where Richard Carlson is in front of the spaceship, the filmmakers built a model of Carlson and of the spaceship. The model of Carlson was about ten inches

(25 centimeters) tall, and the model of the spaceship was about eight feet (2.5 meters) in diameter. When the final scene was shot, it looked as if Carlson's character was being dwarfed by a gigantic alien spacecraft.

In the scene where the avalanche buries the spaceship, the falling "rocks" were actually made out of Styrofoam. To film the scene, the camera was put under a transparent plate so the styrofoam rocks wouldn't damage the lens.

THE SOUND OF THEREMIN

Some of the eerie music in the movie comes from an unusual electronic musical instrument called a theremin. Invented in 1919, a theremin is an electronic box with two long antennae. To produce sound, the musician moves his or her hands around the antennae without actually touching them. The right hand's proximity to one antenna changes the pitch of the sound the theremin is producing, and the left hand's proximity to the other antenna controls the theremin's volume. The spooky sounds produced by theremins have been used in other monster movies, such as *The Day the Earth Stood Still* (1951).

Professor Leon Theremin is pictured here with his 1919 invention. The theremin was the world's first electronic musical instrument, and it is still used today.

Without the digital imaging that today's filmmakers can use, directors in the 1950s had to be creative to produce special effects. One technique they used was filming miniature models. For this scene, the filmmakers created a ten-inch model of Richard Carlson and built an eight-foot model of the alien's spacecraft.

THE MONSTER

Ray Bradbury, Jack Arnold, and William Alland didn't think the monsters should be seen in the movie. They thought the movie would be scarier if moviegoers used their imaginations. They thought the monsters should be so horrible looking that it would be impossible to create an image that would do them justice. So, while the movie was being filmed, smoke was used in place of a monster. The plan was to use the smoke, and spooky music, to signify the appearance of the monsters.

Universal Studios had a different idea. They demanded the monster be shown. A few weeks after Arnold finished shooting the movie, Universal showed the rough movie to art directors. They asked the art directors to make sketches of what the monsters might look like. From the sketches the art directors provided, the studio chose two options. In early April, the makeup department created models based on the sketches. When the models were done, they were photographed in several situations. The studio chose the one-eyed monster seen in the movie. (The model that wasn't chosen was later used in the 1955 movie *This Island Earth*.)

After the model was chosen, the makeup department went to work creating a monster they could use for filming. After filming, the monster was destroyed, probably because the studio wanted details of the movie to remain secret. They didn't want anyone to copy it before the movie was released. Therefore, there is no information remaining on how big the monster was or what materials were used to construct it.

The monster is not shown for long or pictured very clearly. You can see that smoke comes out of its forehead and that it has bulging veins on its forehead and in its eye. The creature's

Because the monster created for *It Came from Outer Space* was destroyed after filming, we don't have detailed information about what materials were used to create it. However, some film historians speculate that its hair was made of glitter and a material called angel hair. Angel hair is spun glass, which was sometimes used to decorate Christmas trees.

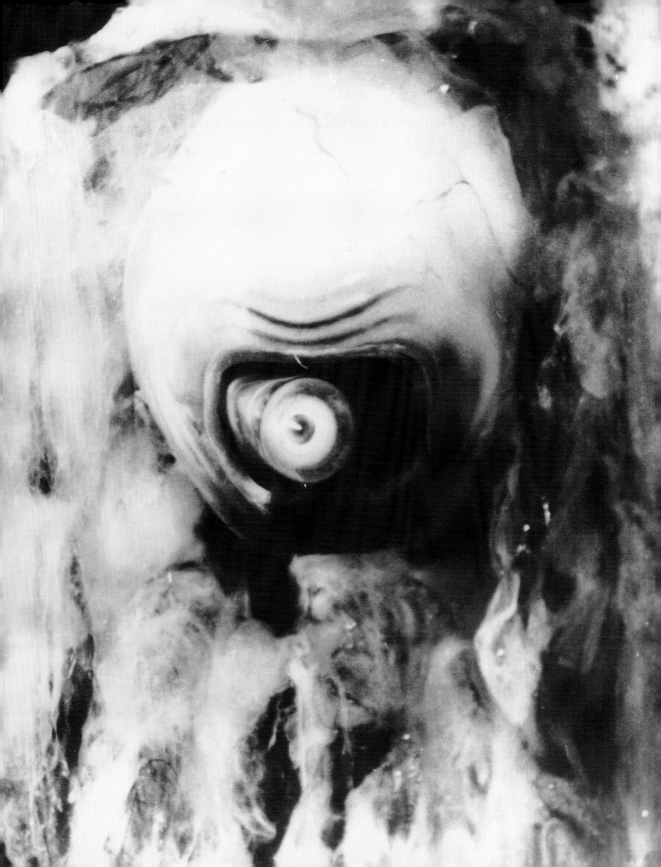

eye was at the end of a stalk that could extend the eye forward to create a 3-D effect.

Because the movie was shot without the monster, the film-makers had to film new scenes after it was created. Five months after the original filming was completed, some of the actors came back to shoot their scenes with the monster. The studio had to add $31,000 to the budget to cover the cost of building the monster and filming new scenes.

THE PREMIERE

When the new monster scenes were completed, the movie was ready for its premiere. On May 26, 1953, the movie made its debut at two theaters in Hollywood, California. Ray Bradbury and about sixty other celebrities attended the premiere at the Pantages Theater. At the RKO Hill Street Theater, Russell Johnson and other stars viewed the completed movie for the first time.

There was a lot of publicity for the movie. Most of the publicity was focused on the fact that the movie was in 3-D. The movie posters proclaimed that the movie featured "Thrills that almost touch you through the magic of 3-Dimension," and "Amazing sights the human eye has never before seen!" Three-dimensional movies were doing very well at the box office, and *It Came from Outer Space* was no exception. The movie made a lot of money in its first week and continued to make money in the weeks following the premiere. The movie cost about $532,000 (the equivalent of about $3.7 million in 2005) to make and earned about $6.5 million (about $45 million in 2005).

The movie poster for *It Came from Outer Space* focused on the fact that the film was in 3-D, which was incredibly popular at the time the movie was made. However, *It Came from Outer Space* didn't overdo the 3-D effects. Instead, it relied on strong performances and a gripping plot.

Although the public liked the movie, film reviewers were not as kind. However, many reviewers wrote that they liked the 3-D effects.

Barbara Rush won a Golden Globe award for Most Promising Female Newcomer for her role in the movie. *It Came from Outer Space* was nominated for a Hugo Award for Best Dramatic Presentation, but it did not win.

CHAPTER 3

ORIGINS OF THE STORY

Science fiction examines how science and technology have an impact on people and the world that they live in. Some science fiction sticks closer to the facts than others. However, all science fiction movies allow us to visit new worlds. We can go far into the future or travel back into the distant past.

The first science fiction movie was made in 1902. Filmed by a French man named Georges Méliès, it was called *A Trip to the Moon*. Under twenty minutes in length, *A Trip to the Moon* had a very basic plot. The film also had some very early special effects. The effects were not impressive by today's standards, but they were very innovative for the time.

Méliès pioneered a process known as stop-motion photography. He would start filming and then stop the camera. While the camera was off, he would move the people or things being filmed, and then he would restart the camera. Méliès created a great number of imaginative effects by using this simple procedure.

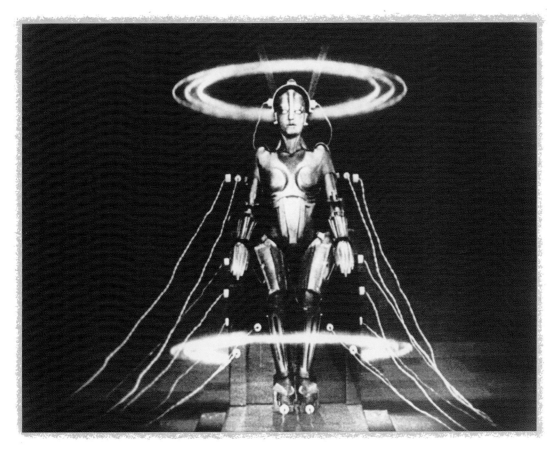

This scene from *Metropolis* (1927) shows the robot version of the heroine Maria. Some film historians have speculated that George Lucas modeled C3PO, the droid from his *Star Wars* movies, after this robot. *Metropolis* influenced many other science fiction movies that followed it.

The next notable science fiction movie was called *Metropolis*, and it premiered in 1927. Directed by Fritz Lang, the movie was set in a futuristic city in which the workers are slaves to the machines that run the city. A girl named Maria tries to get the workers to revolt against the machines. The people who own the city get a scientist to build a robot that looks exactly

FROM OUT OF SPACE....
A WARNING AND AN ULTIMATUM!
THE DAY THE EARTH STOOD STILL
WITH
MICHAEL RENNIE · PATRICIA NEAL · HUGH MARLOWE
SAM JAFFE · BILLY GRAY · FRANCES BAVIER · LOCK MARTIN
PRODUCED BY
JULIAN BLAUSTEIN
DIRECTED BY
ROBERT WISE
EDMUND H. NORTH
20th CENTURY-FOX

like Maria. The robot creates a riot in the city, which is nearly destroyed. Eventually the real Maria saves the day, and the film resolves peacefully.

INVADERS FROM SPACE

By the late 1940s, science fiction films were commonplace. One reason for this new focus on science fiction was a sudden public interest in creatures from outer space. In 1947, an unidentified flying object, or UFO, was spotted in Washington State. The American public was very interested in what the object might be. Many more sightings followed. The idea that Earth may be visited by creatures from other planets inspired writers and filmmakers.

One of the first movies about visitors from outer space was the 1951 movie *The Day the Earth Stood Still*. In this movie, as in *It Came from Outer Space*, the alien visitor comes in peace. Because they do not understand the alien, the people of Earth kill it.

The Thing from Another World, also made in 1951, was another movie about alien visitors. This time, however, the alien does not come in peace. Although humans eventually kill the

The Day the Earth Stood Still (1951) featured the alien Klaatu, who arrives in Washington, D.C., in a flying saucer. Klaatu tries to bring a message of peace to the world. To get everyone to listen and to demonstrate his power, he stops everything run by electricity. Despite his message of peace, the people of Earth are threatened by his message and by his power, and eventually kill him.

During the 1950s, many Americans were concerned about the possibility of a nuclear attack. Cities and towns created official fallout shelters, which could protect people from the aftereffects of radiation. Many families set up their own fallout shelters in basements and other underground locations. The Walter Kiddie Nuclear Laboratories, Inc., designed a fallout shelter, pictured above, to protect families for up to five days.

alien, at the end of the movie a warning flashes on the screen: "Watch the sky. They're coming." Many other movies featuring unfriendly alien visitors, such as 1953's *The War of the Worlds*, were made around this time.

FEAR OF THE UNKNOWN

One factor contributing to the explosion of science fiction films in the late 1940s and early 1950s was the Cold War (1947–1991). The Cold War was principally a conflict between the United States and the Soviet Union. Although they had been allies during World War II, the two superpowers soon became rivals. The Cold War never resulted in direct, armed conflict between the two nations, but both countries had large militaries and nuclear weapons, and it was a tense time.

The 1956 film *Invasion of the Body Snatchers*, directed by Don Siegel, featured aliens who could assume human form. By replacing one person after another, they eventually take over a small California town. In this scene, the characters Dr. Miles Bennell (Kevin McCarthy) and Dana Wynter (Becky Driscoll) flee from the invaders.

This rivalry stemmed from the fact that the Soviet Union was a Communist country and the United States was not. At the time, Americans had strong feelings against Communism. There was a lot that the United States found strange and alien about Russia and its system of government, and this fear of the unknown fed many of the science fiction movies of the time. An example of this is 1956's

Invasion of the Body Snatchers. In this movie, the aliens assume the forms of human hosts, who then die. The aliens slowly take over a small California town, and soon it is impossible to tell who is human and who is an alien. Many people saw this film as a movie about Communism taking over the United States. *Invasion of the Body Snatchers* can also be interpreted as a commentary on conformity in general.

It Came from Outer Space had a different message than many science fiction movies of the time. Jack Arnold wanted to say that human beings fear and hate things that are different from themselves. According to Arnold, we won't be ready to welcome visitors from another world until we can progress beyond these prejudices.

CHAPTER 4

BEYOND IT CAME FROM OUTER SPACE

After *It Came from Outer Space*, some of the cast and crew went on to make other science fiction movies. Jack Arnold directed *Creature from the Black Lagoon* (1954), *Revenge of the Creature* (1955), and *The Incredible Shrinking Man* (1957). Richard Carlson worked with Arnold again as the star of *Creature from the Black Lagoon*. He starred in other monster movies, including *The Magnetic Monster* (1953) and *The Maze* (1953). He also directed a monster movie in 1954 called *Riders to the Stars*.

Barbara Rush starred in many films in the 1950s and later appeared in television shows like *All My Children* and *7th Heaven*. She lives in California and is still acting.

In the 1960s and 1970s, Arnold directed episodes of television shows like *The Brady Bunch* and *Gilligan's Island*. Russell Johnson, who starred as George in *It Came from Outer Space*, acted in other movies in the 1950s. He is best known for playing the Professor on the television show *Gilligan's Island*, which ran from 1964 to 1967.

A year after *It Came from Outer Space* was released, Jack Arnold *(far right)* directed another 3-D movie, also starring Richard Carlson *(second from left)*. *The Creature from the Black Lagoon* was set in the jungle surrounding the Amazon River, where a team of scientists hunting for fossils discovers an ancient monster living in the river. The monster captures the only woman with the team, and the other scientists must rescue her. Today, *The Creature from the Black Lagoon* is considered to be a classic.

Ray Bradbury continues to write science fiction stories and books. Because of the success of his work on *It Came from Outer Space*, he wrote several screenplays, including *Moby Dick* in 1956. He also adapted his novel *Something Wicked This Way Comes* into a movie in 1983.

REISSUES AND REMAKES

In 1972, *It Came from Outer Space* was rereleased in theaters in 3-D. In 1980 it was released as a home video. However, there were problems transferring the 3-D movie to video. The quality of the video was so bad that it was nearly unwatchable. The company that released it, MCA, finally had to stop selling the tapes. In 2002, Universal released a two-dimensional version of the movie on DVD. *It Came from Outer Space* can sometimes be seen in 3-D at 3-D film festivals.

Although *It Came from Outer Space* has not been remade, there is a 1996 television movie called *It Came from Outer Space II*. It originally aired on the Sci-Fi channel. This sequel

UPDATING THE CLASSICS

Several movies popular in the 1950s have been remade numerous times. Two good examples are *Invasion of the Body Snatchers* and *The War of the Worlds*. *Invasion of the Body Snatchers* was remade in 1978 and 1993, and another version is currently in production. *The War of the Worlds* was adapted as a TV series in 1988, and Steven Spielberg remade the movie in 2005.

In 1996, Roger Duchowny directed a made-for-television sequel to *It Came from Outer Space*. In the television version, a cloud descends over a desert town. As in the original movie, the aliens take over the bodies of the townspeople.

In Steven Spielberg's *Close Encounters of the Third Kind* (1977), the aliens in the movie come in peace, although they abduct many people from Earth. The main character of the film, played by Richard Dreyfuss, is an electrical lineman. This is a reference to George and Frank, the telephone linemen in *It Came from Outer Space*. In a scene from the end of the film, a giant alien ship descends and the aliens return the humans they had abducted.

is built on the same basic plot of the original, but it is set in the 1990s. The special effects in the sequel are more advanced, but most critics agree that the original movie was far superior.

THE INFLUENCE OF *IT CAME FROM OUTER SPACE*

Many filmmakers were influenced by what they saw in *It Came from Outer Space*. For example, Steven Spielberg says that he made one of his biggest hit movies because he saw *It Came from Outer Space* when he was a child. Spielberg's 1977 movie *Close Encounters of the Third Kind* was directly inspired by *It Came from Outer Space*.

On the *It Came from Outer Space* DVD commentary, film historian Tom Weaver tells what happened when Ray Bradbury met Steven Spielberg at the premiere of *Close Encounters of the Third Kind*. When the movie was over, Bradbury told Spielberg how much he liked the movie. Spielberg replied, "How did you like *your* film? *Close Encounters* wouldn't have been born if I hadn't seen *It Came from Outer Space* six times when I was a kid. Thanks."

It Came from Outer Space didn't win many awards, but it thrilled audiences with its exciting 3-D effects. Its message— that we should not fear things just because they are different from us—is still important today.

FILMOGRAPHY

It Came From Outer Space (1953)   Directed by Jack Arnold with a story by Ray Bradbury, and starring Barbara Rush and Richard Carlson, this film was the first science fiction movie shot in 3–D. The movie would go on to influence dozens of science fiction films.

It Came from Outer Space II (TV movie, 1996) This made-for-television movie was based on the original movie, with some differences in the plot.

Besides *It Came From Outer Space* and its sequel, there have been a number of other movies dealing with invaders from another planet.

The Day the Earth Stood Still (1951) The alien Klaatu comes to Earth in peace but is killed by fearful humans.

The Thing from Another World (1951) A dangerous alien is discovered buried in the ice at an Arctic research station. After the alien is bought back to the research station, it thaws out and goes on a rampage

The War of the Worlds (1953) Based on an H. G. Wells novel about a martian invasion of Earth, *War of the Worlds* would be remade by Steven Spielberg in 2005.

Earth vs. the Flying Saucers (1956) Invading aliens attack London, Paris, and Moscow before being defeated in the skies above Washington, D.C.

Invasion of the Body Snatchers (1956)   Aliens take over human bodies and become perfect copies of the human hosts, killing them in the process. *Invasion of the Body Snatchers* was remade in 1978 and 1993.

The Blob (1958) A gooey alien life-form arrives on Earth in a meteor and devours anything in its path. *The Blob* was remade in 1988.

Close Encounters of the Third Kind (1977) Strange happenings draw people into the desert for a meeting with aliens. Director Steven Spielberg has cited *It Came From Outer Space* as being a major influence on *Close Encounters of the Third Kind.*

Signs (2002). Mysterious crop circles appear around the world. Many people think that the crop circles are just an elaborate prank, but it turns out that they were created by aliens who are planning to invade Earth.

GLOSSARY

antenna A device for sending or receiving radio waves.

art director The head of an art department. In the film industry, this usually includes the makeup and special effects departments.

avalanche A large mass of earth, rock, or snow that slides down a mountain or cliff.

catapult A device that can launch objects into the air.

cavern A cave.

debut A first public appearance.

dialogue The conversation between characters in a movie or play.

director A person who guides, or directs, the filming of a movie.

eerie Spooky.

hexagon A geometric shape with six sides.

inexpressive Not reflecting feeling or emotion.

lineman Someone who sets up and repairs power or telephone lines.

meteor Matter from space that glows as it enters Earth's atmosphere; often referred to as a shooting star.

mine A pit or tunnel from which minerals (such as coal, gold, or diamonds) are extracted.

prejudice Unfriendly feelings directed against an individual or a group.

premiere The first showing of a movie.

producer A person who supervises or finances a movie.

recruit To hire workers.

screenplay A written story prepared for film production.

sound stage A large building or room that is soundproof, usually inside a movie studio.

studio A place where motion pictures are made.

survey To look over; to gather information about.

treatment A short overview of the plot of a movie, which can be expanded into a screenplay.

FOR MORE INFORMATION

American Film Institute
2021 N. Western Avenue
Los Angeles, CA 90027-1657
(323) 856-7600
Web site: http://www.afi.com

Science Fiction Museum and Hall of Fame
325 5th Avenue N.
Seattle, WA 98109
(206) 724-3428
Web site: http://www.sfhomeworld.org/

Universal Studios
100 Universal City Plaza
Universal City, CA 91608
(818) 508-9600
Web site: http://www.universalstudios.com/index.php

WEB SITES

Due to the changing nature of Internet links, the Rosen Publishing Group, Inc., has developed an online list of Web sites related to the subject of this book. This site is updated regularly. Please use this link to access the list:

http://www.rosenlinks.com/famm/icfos

FOR FURTHER READING

Edelson, Edward. *Visions of Tomorrow: Great Science Fiction from the Movies*. Garden City, NY: Doubleday & Company, 1975.

Pinteau, Pascal. *Special Effects: An Oral History*. New York, NY: Harry N. Abrams, 2005.

Pringle, David. *The Ultimate Encyclopedia of Science Fiction: The Definitive Illustrated Guide.* London, England: Carlton Books, 1997.

Richards, Gregory B. *Science Fiction Movies*. Greenwich, CT: Bison Books, 1984.

Thorne, Ian. *It Came from Outer Space*. Mankato, MN: Crestwood House, 1982.

BIBLIOGRAPHY

Edelson, Edward. *Visions of Tomorrow: Great Science Fiction from the Movies*. Garden City, NY: Doubleday & Company, 1975.

Haining, Peter, ed. *Vintage Science Fiction*. New York, NY: Carroll & Graf Publishers, 1999.

Hayes, R. M. *3-D Movies: A History and Filmography of Stereoscopic Cinema*. Jefferson, NC: McFarland & Company: 1989.

Pringle, David. *The Ultimate Encyclopedia of Science Fiction: The Definitive Illustrated Guide*. London, England: Carlton Books, 1997.

Richards, Gregory B. *Science Fiction Movies*. Greenwich, CT: Bison Books, 1984.

Skal, David J. "The Universe According to Universal." Disc 1. *It Came from Outer Space*. DVD. Universal City, CA: Universal Studios: 2002.

Weaver, Tom. *Attack of the Monster Movie Makers: Interviews with 20 Genre Greats*. Jefferson, NC: McFarland & Company: 1994.

Weaver, Tom. "Commentary." Disc 1. *It Came from Outer Space*. DVD. Universal City, CA: Universal Studios: 2002.

INDEX

ABOUT THE AUTHOR

Simone Payment has a bachelor's degree in psychology from Cornell University and a master's degree in elementary education from Wheelock College. She is the author of fourteen books for young adults. Her book *Inside Special Operations: Navy SEALs* (also from Rosen Publishing) was selected as one of the American Library Association's 2004 Quick Picks for Reluctant Young Readers and is on the Nonfiction Honor List of Voice of Youth Advocates. She grew up watching monster movies on Saturday afternoons and was lucky to see *It Came from Outer Space* in its original 3-D form at a 3-D movie festival in 2005.

PHOTO CREDITS

Cover, pp. 1, 4, 8, 11, 12, 14, 15, 17, 22, 23, 25, 28, 30, 35, 36, 37 © Photofest; pp. 6, 18, 27, 33, 38 Everett Collection; pp. 29, 32 © Bettmann/Corbis.

Designer: Thomas Forget